MENOPAWS

{The Silent Meow}

This book is dedicated to Ed,
who was always there with love and encouragement.

Acknowledgments:
Many thanks to Andy, Michael, and Jack.
Many more to my cats, my kids, and my publisher.

MENOPAWS

{The Silent Meow}

by Martha Sacks

Illustrations by Jack E. Davis

Ten Speed Press
Berkeley, California

Ten Speed Press
P.O. Box 7123
Berkeley, CA 94707

Designed and Art Directed by Rey international
Edited by Andy Meisler
Printed in Hong Kong through Phoenix Offset

**Library of Congress
Cataloging-in-Publication Data**

Sacks, Martha.
Menopaws: the silent meow
by Martha Sacks; illustrated by Jack E. Davis
p. cm.   ISBN 0-89815-780-3 (pbk.: alk. paper)
1. Cats – Caricature and cartoons
2. Menopause – Caricature and cartoons
I. Davis, Jack E.   II. Title
PN6727.S15M46   1994
741.5 973 – dc20
95-17881   CIP

8   9   10 — 99   98   97

INTRODUCTION

Becoming a mature female is a natural – and, yes –
even pleasurable experience. This universal
adventure is to be welcomed, not feared.

True, there will be some adjustments. But keep
your head held high. Although some doors are
closing, others are opening. This is an exciting
passageway to the future.

Know your options. Ease the transitions. Remember!
These can be the best years of your lives.

PART I

YOUR BODY

8

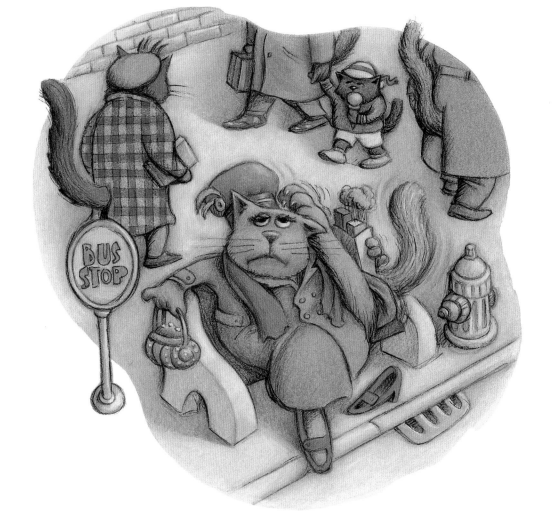

SYMPTOM Dry, itchy, flaky skin

Ace
MILK

REMEDY **Milk baths**

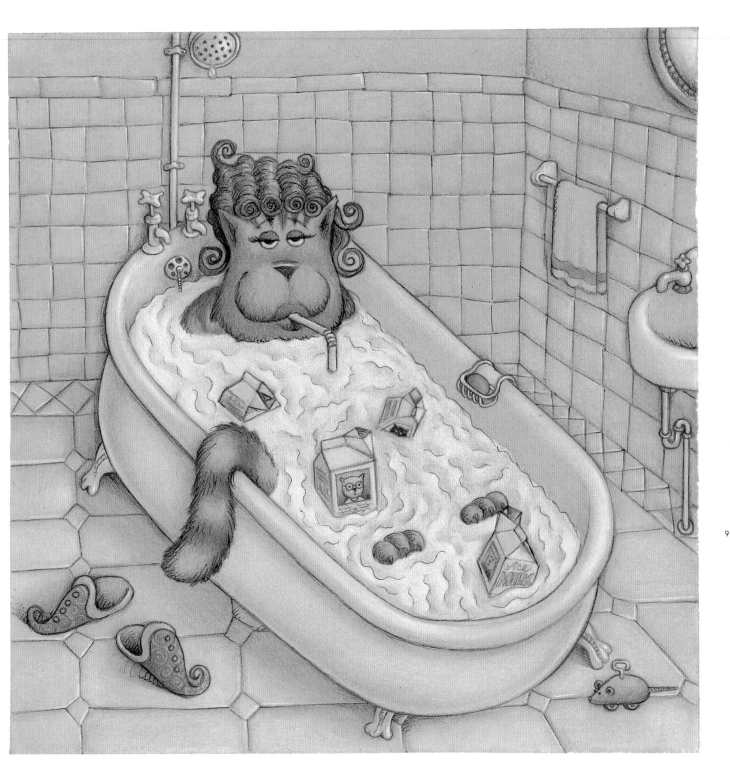

SYMPTOM Hot flashes

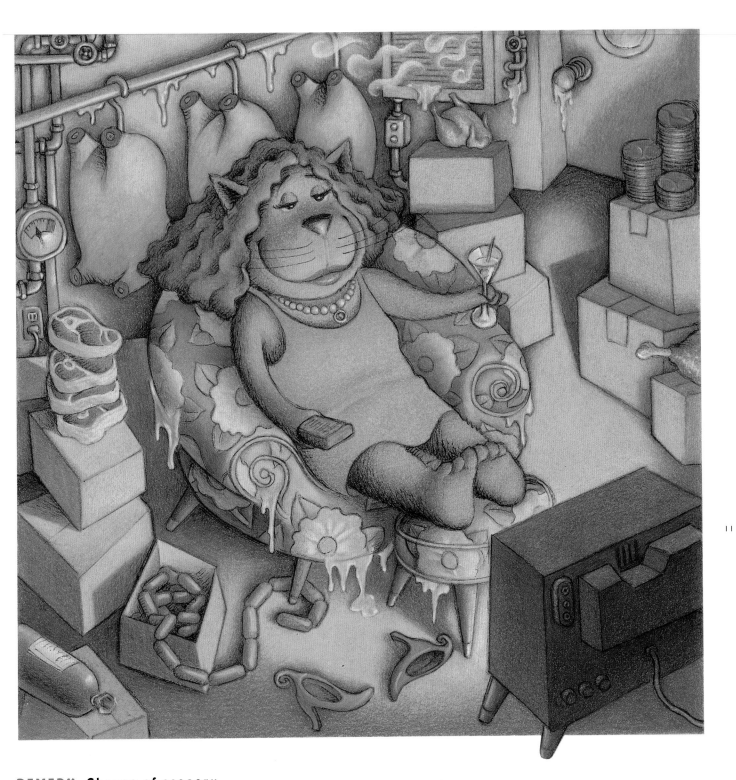

REMEDY Change of scenery

TV
Call Now!
RICHARD
SIMMONS
215-1859
A Fat Girls
Phone never
Rings

SYMPTOM **Weight gain**

Fat★Fabulous★Fluffy
QUEEN SIZED

REMEDY **Acceptance**

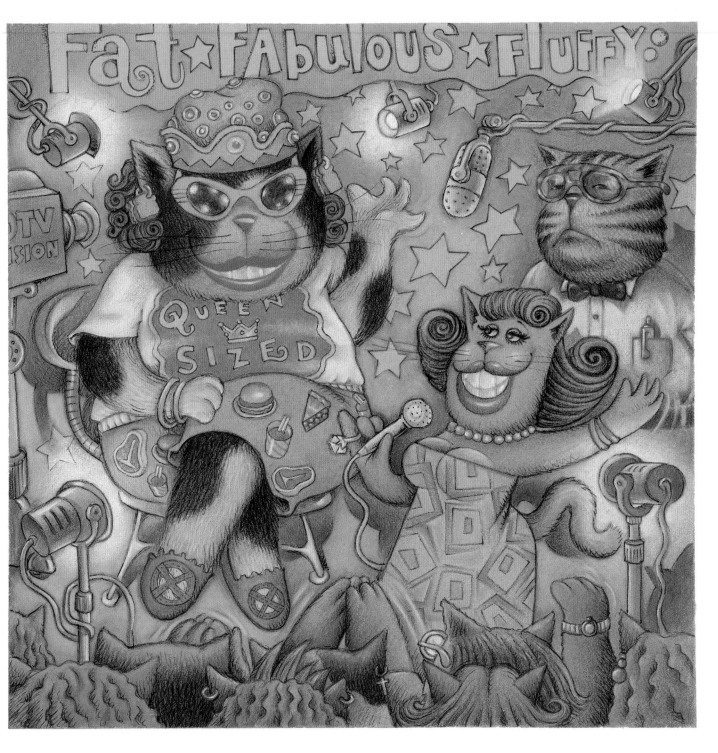

SYMPTOM Weight loss

REMEDY Celebration

SYMPTOM Night sweats

17

REMEDY Sleep naked

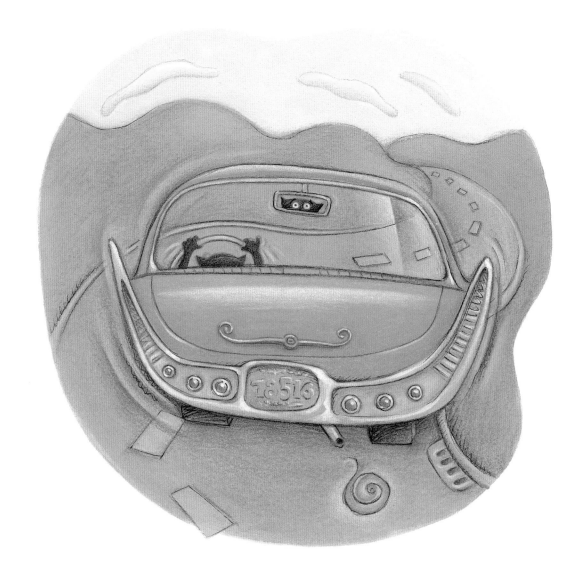

SYMPTOM **Loss of height**

19

REMEDY New shoes

20

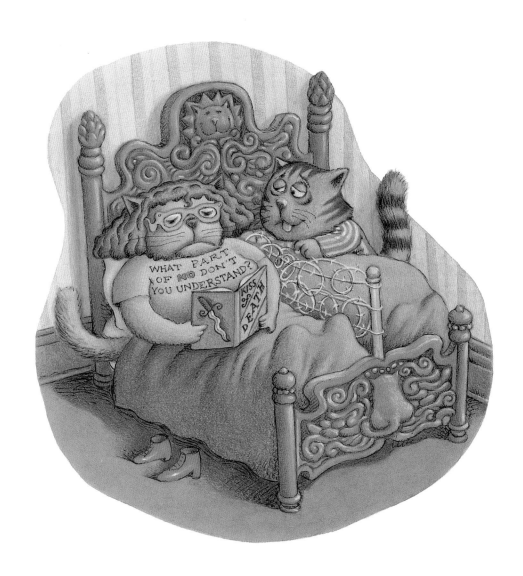

SYMPTOM Decreased sexual desire

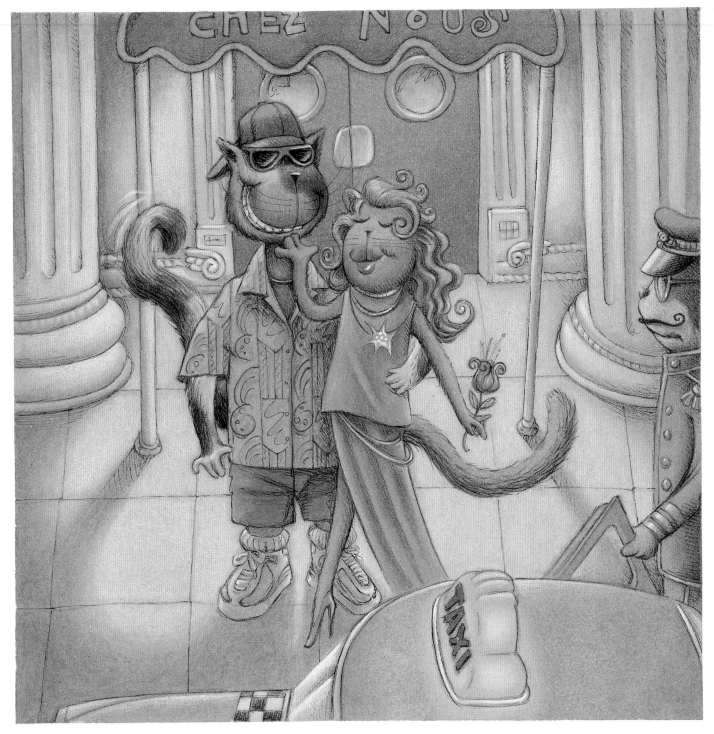

REMEDY **Younger boyfriend**

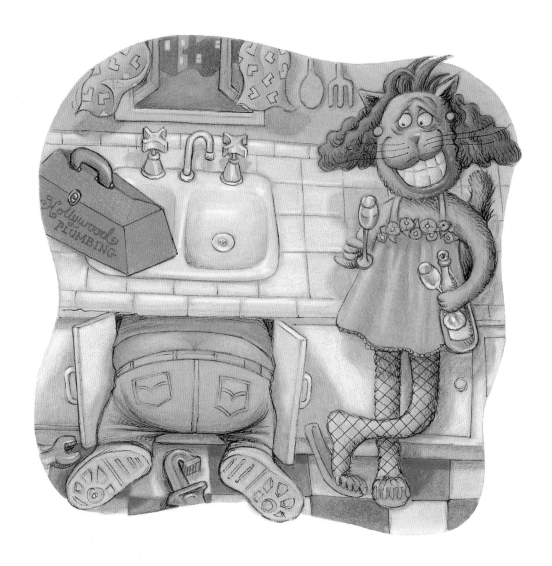

SYMPTOM Increased sexual desire

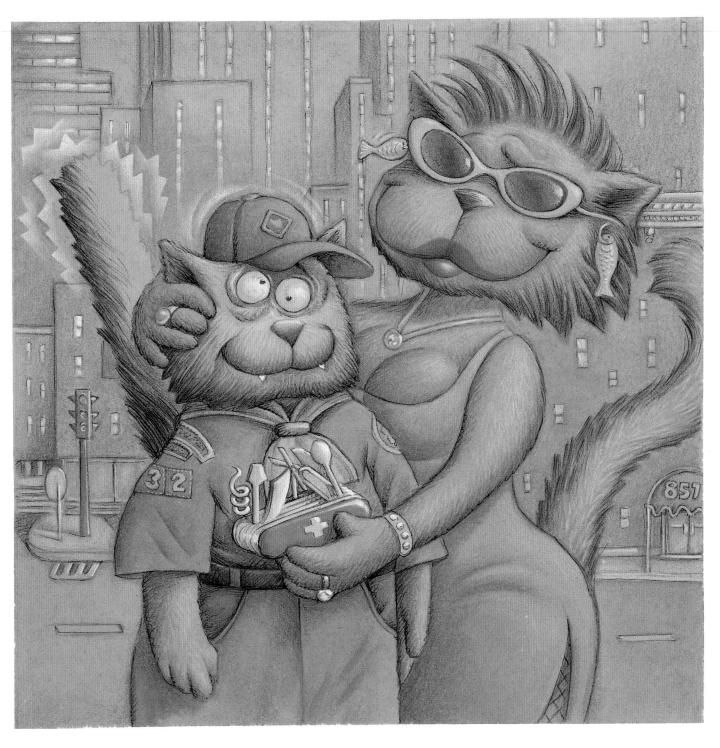

REMEDY **Younger boyfriend**

PART II

YOUR MIND

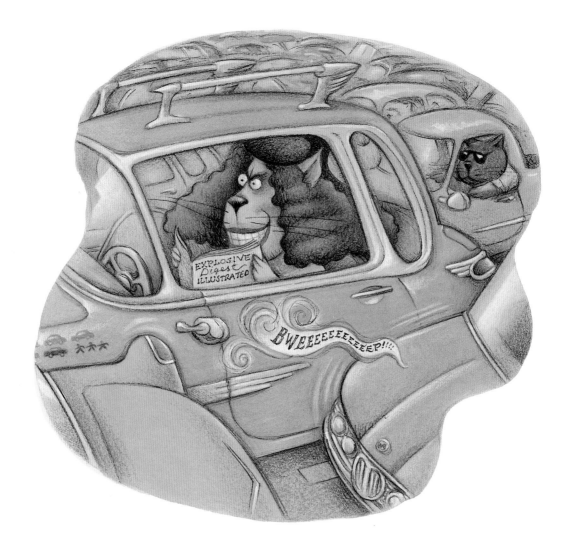

DIFFICULTY Impatience

$41.
ANUT
YUMMIES
CAT Snackers
CAT Snackers
PRUNE JUICE 89

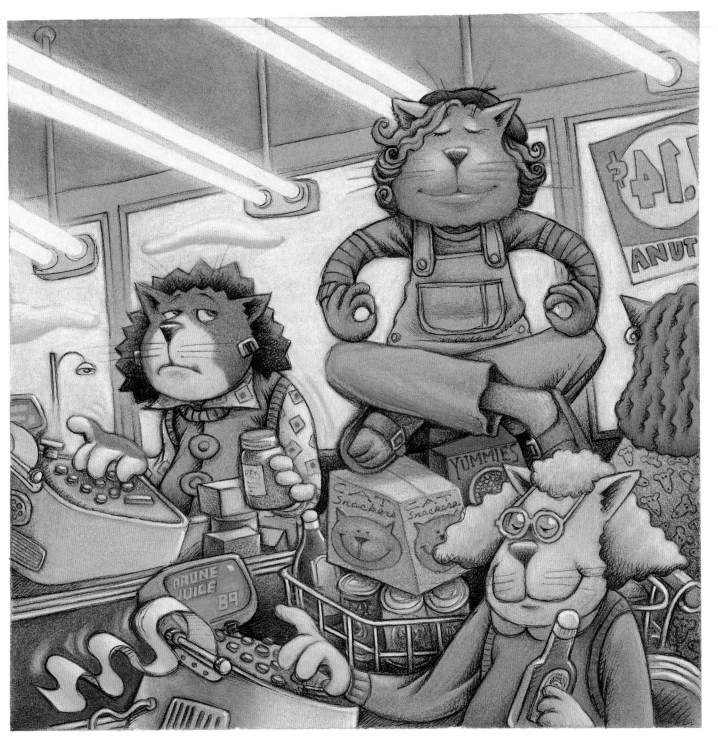

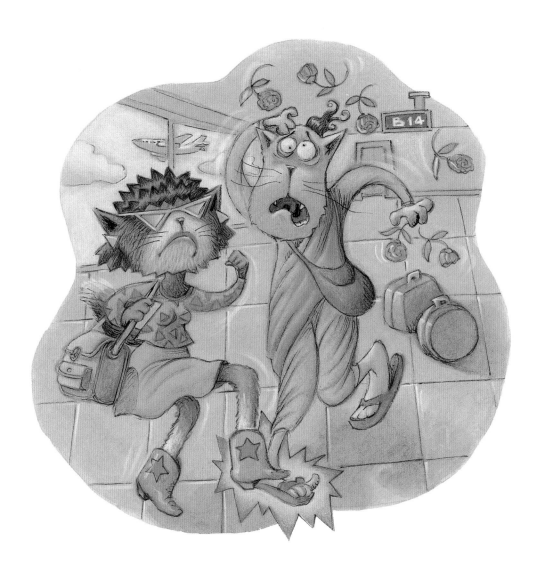

DIFFICULTY Irritability

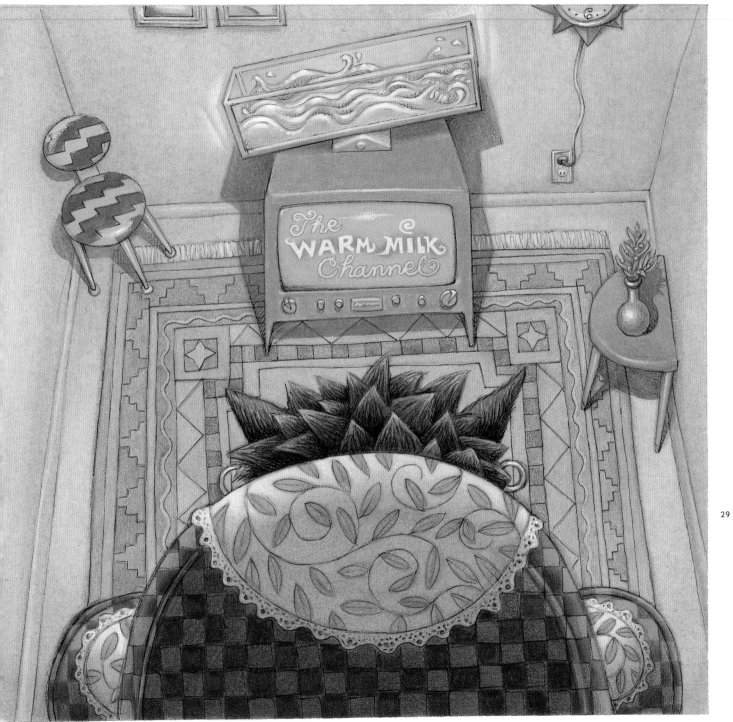

29

STRATEGY Relaxation techniques

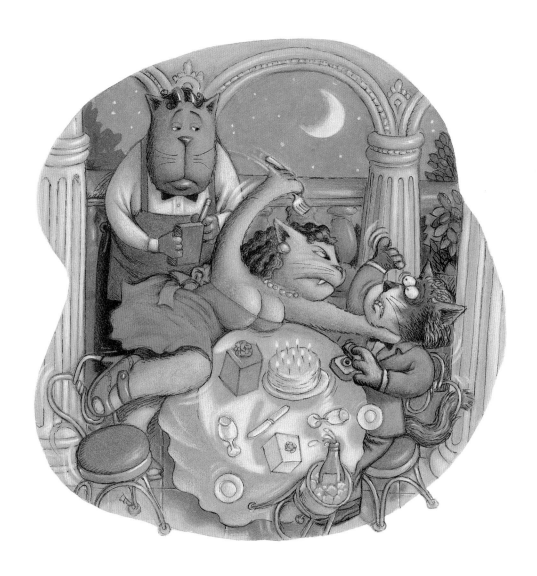

DIFFICULTY Mood swings

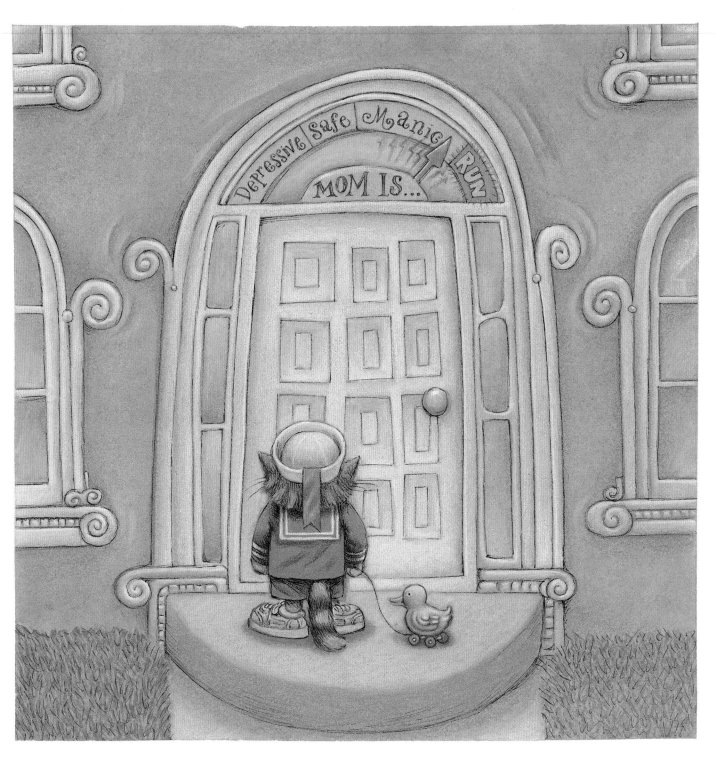

31

STRATEGY **Better communication**

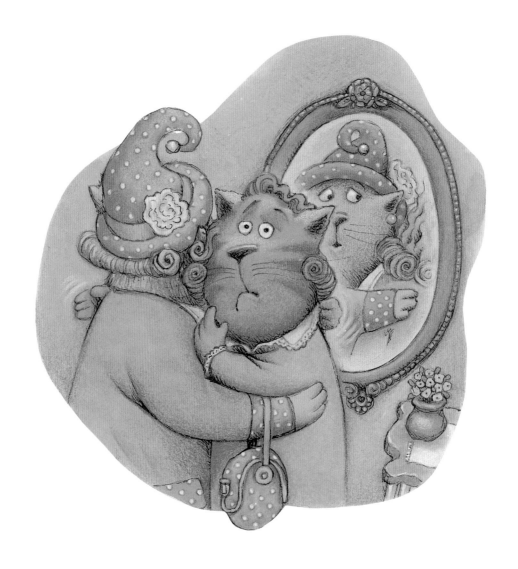

DIFFICULTY Short term memory loss

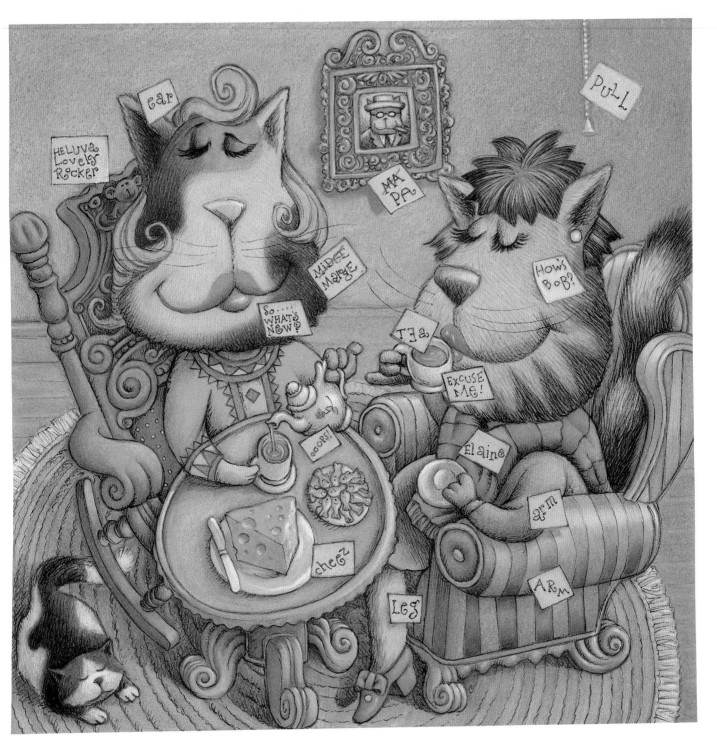

33

STRATEGY Short term memory aids

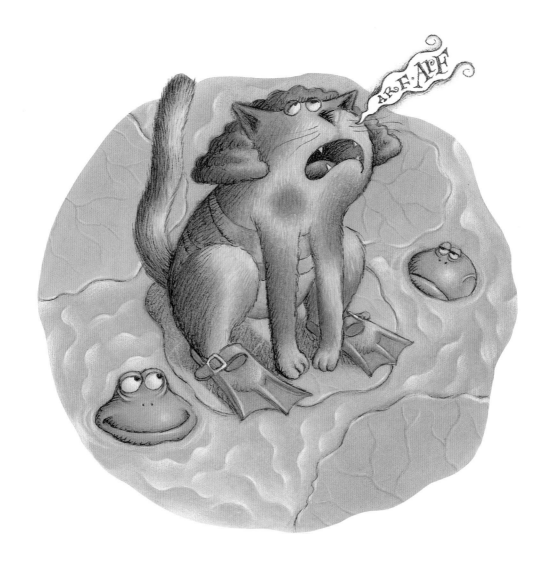

DIFFICULTY Identity crisis

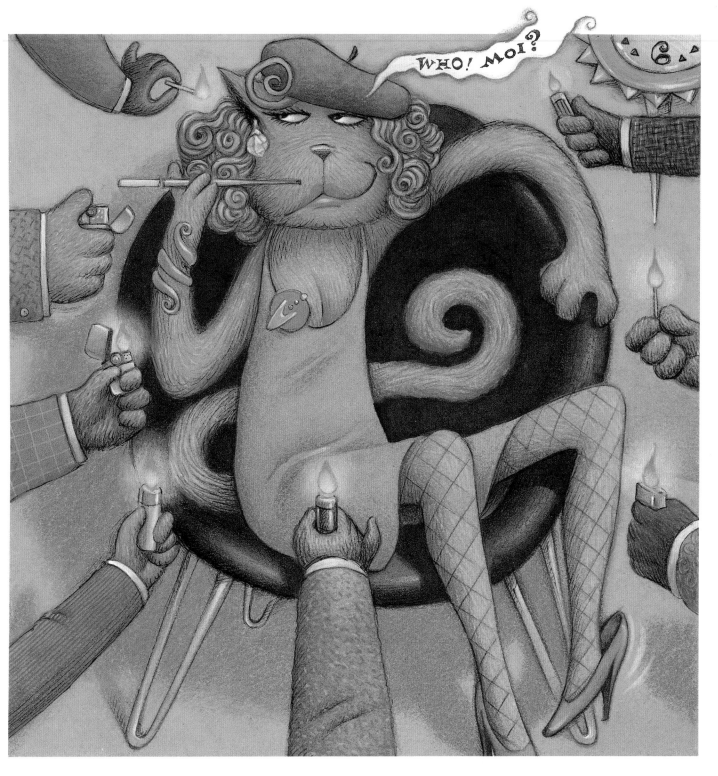

STRATEGY Develop foreign accent for interest

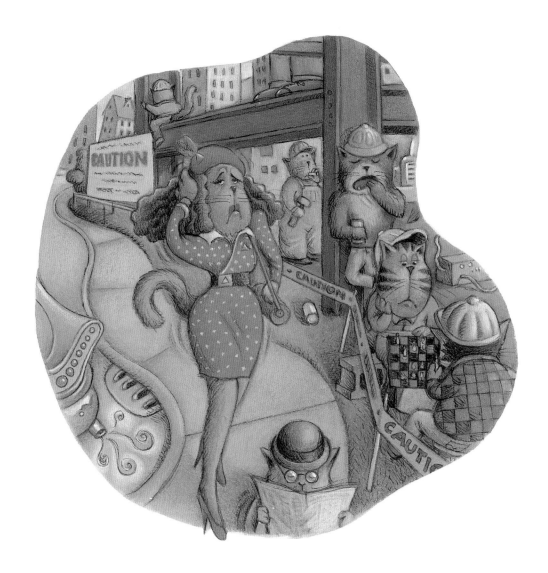

DIFFICULTY Perceived loss of femininity

STRATEGY **New lingerie**

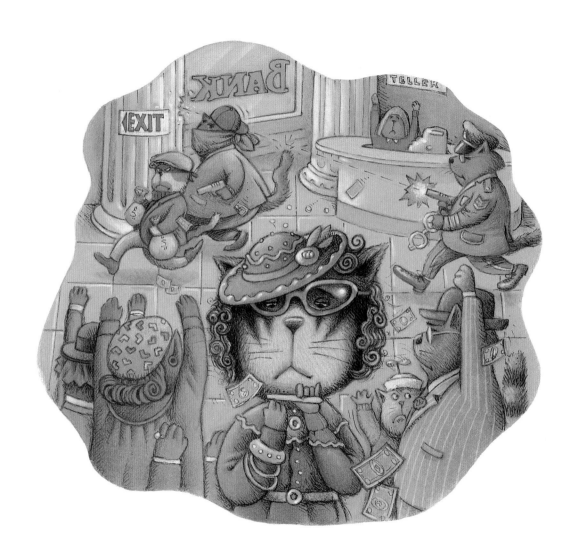

DIFFICULTY Lack of concentration

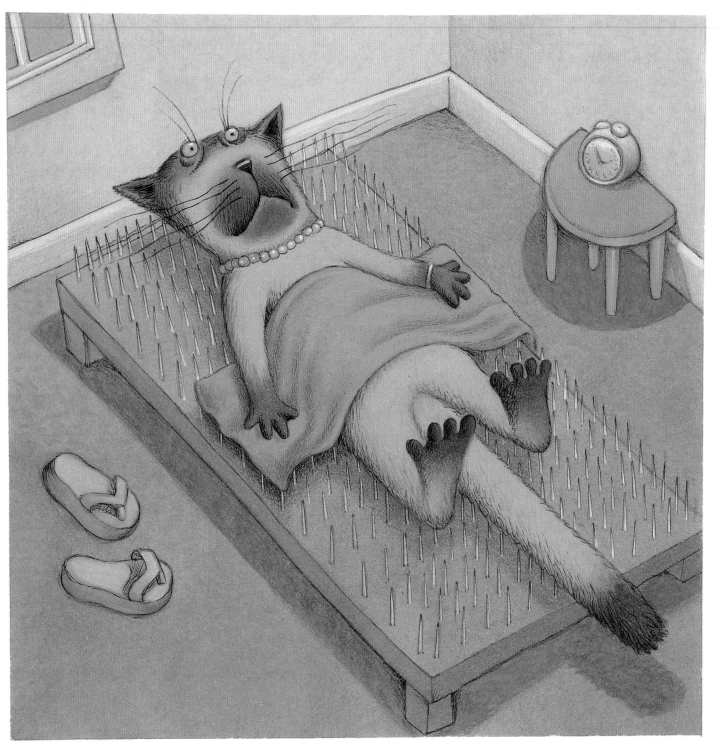

39

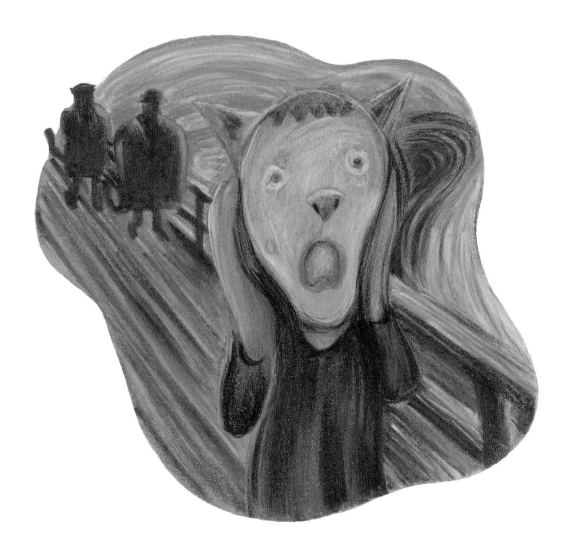

DIFFICULTY Depression

STRATEGY Shopping

PART III

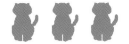

YOUR LIFESTYLE

PROBLEM Boredom

Beginning
TAXIDERMY
~by~
Dr. H. Hyde
GLUE

SOLUTION **New hobbies**

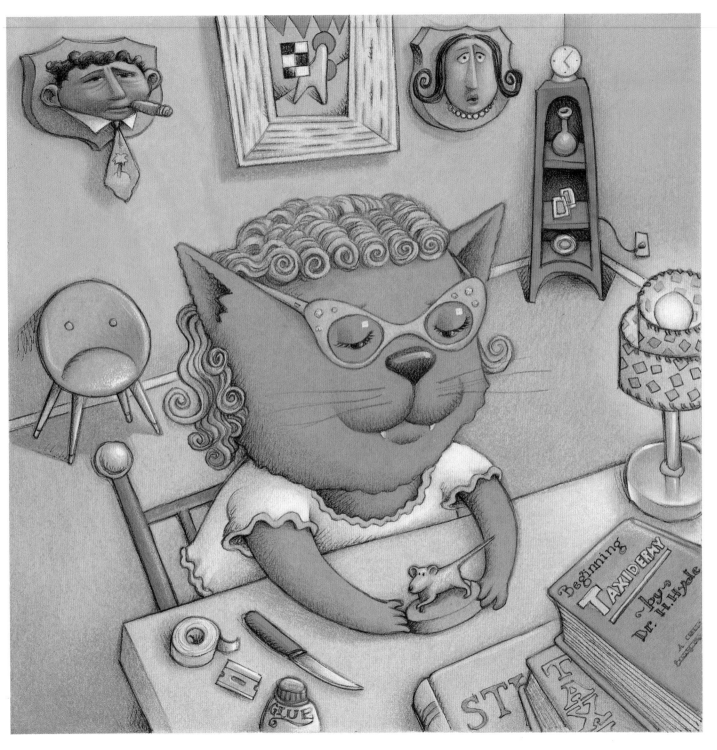

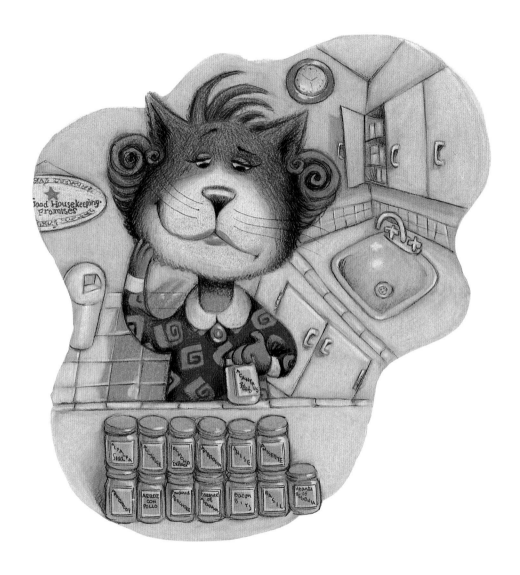

PROBLEM Pointless perfectionism

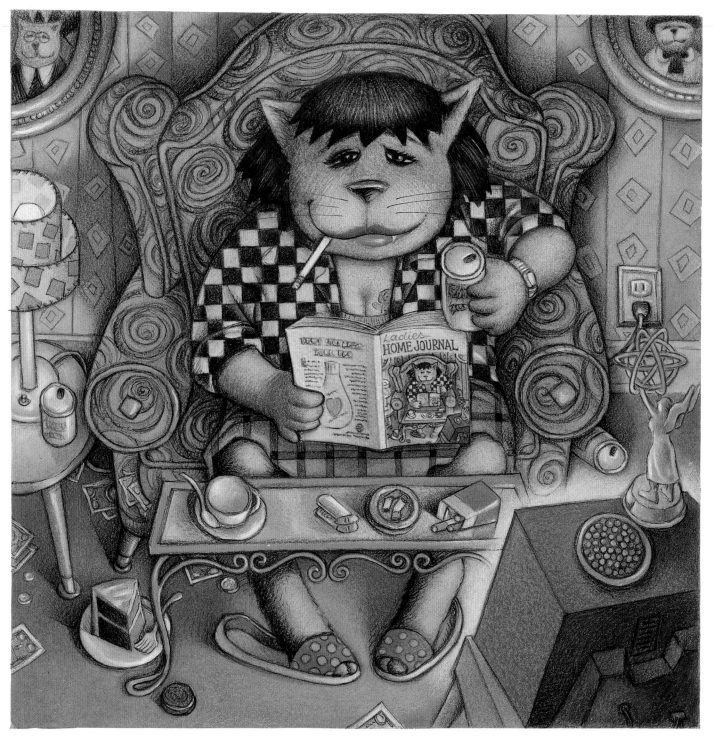

SOLUTION Search out new role models

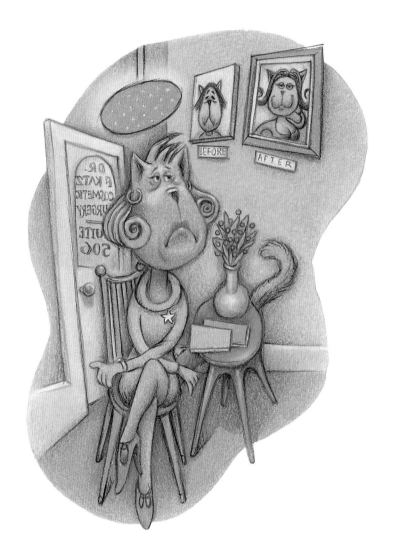

PROBLEM Obsession with youthful appearance

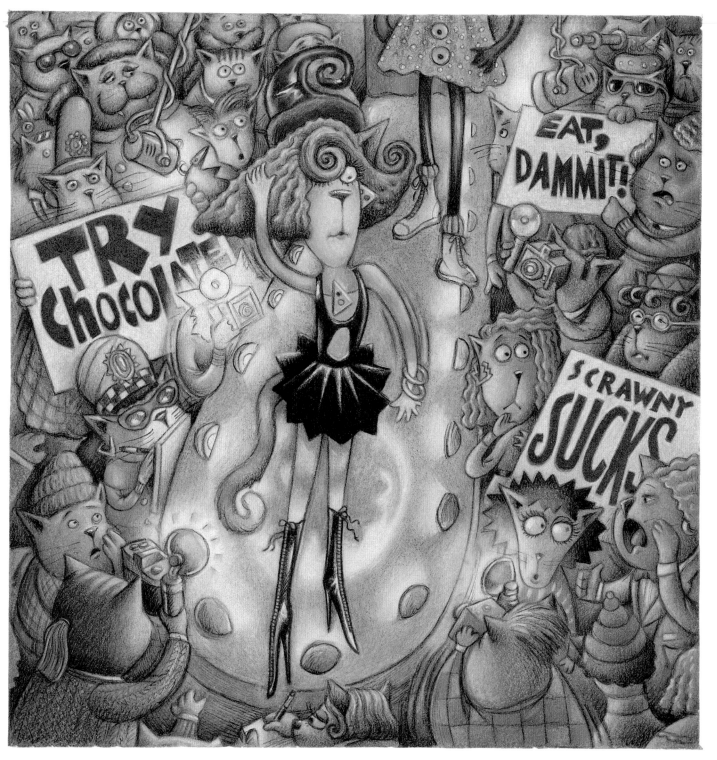

SOLUTION Boycott mass media

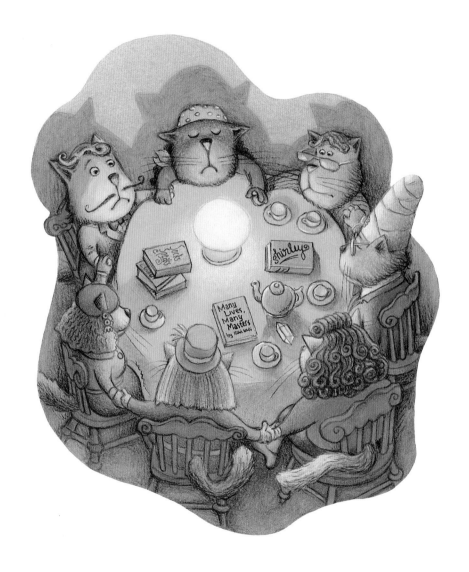

PROBLEM Obsession with the occult

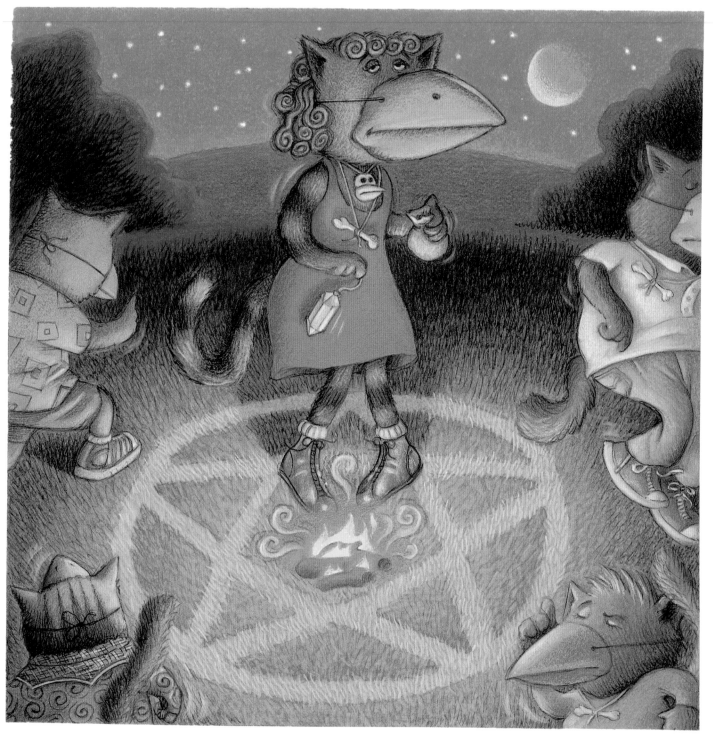

51

SOLUTION Total immersion

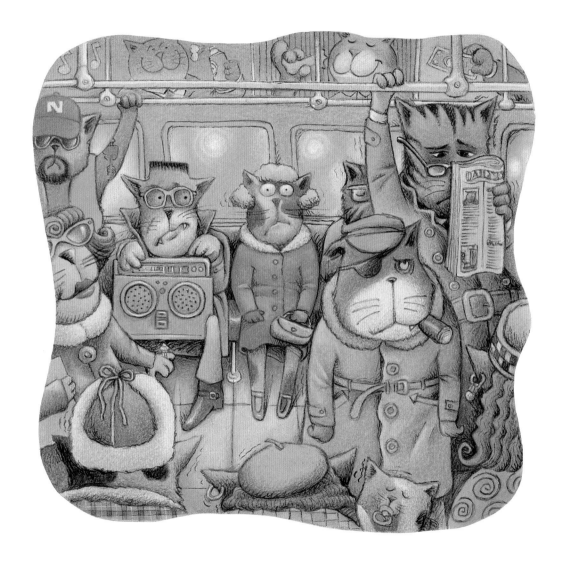

PROBLEM Desire for inner peace

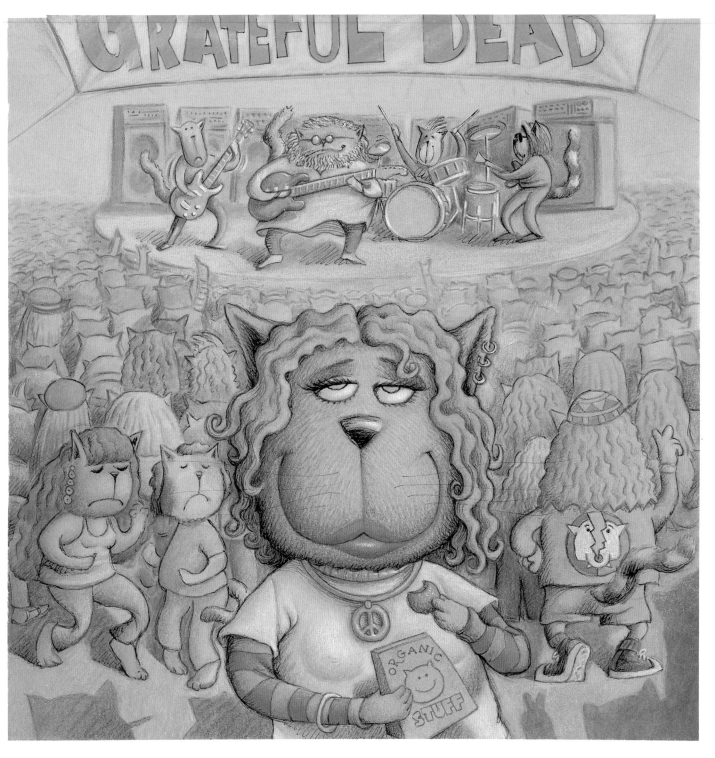

SOLUTION **Rediscover mainstream religion**

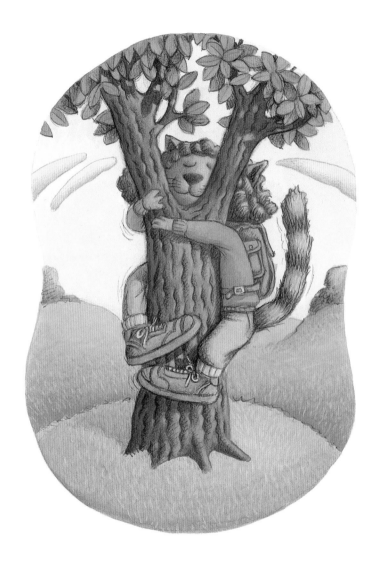

PROBLEM Urge to bond with nature

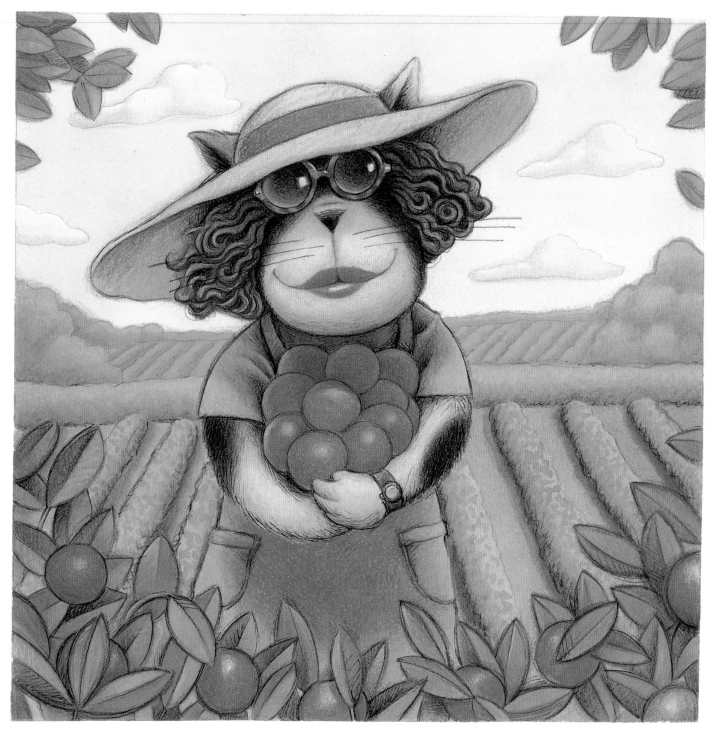

SOLUTION **Plant veggie garden**

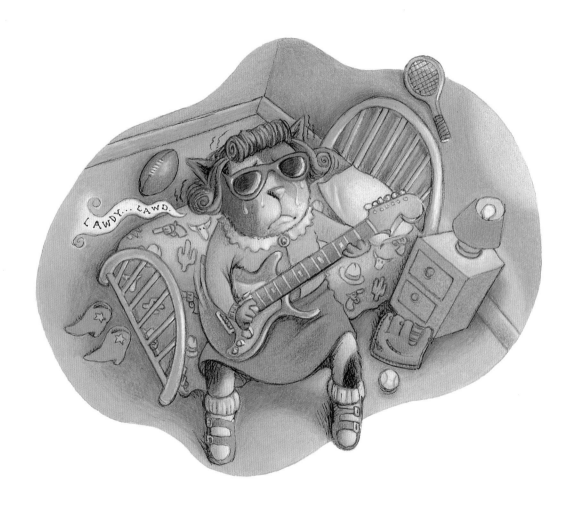

PROBLEM Empty nest syndrome

SOLUTION Adoption

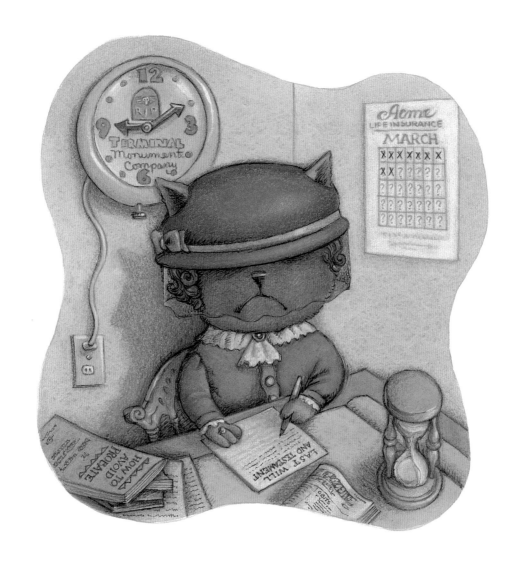

58

PROBLEM Irrational fear of the future

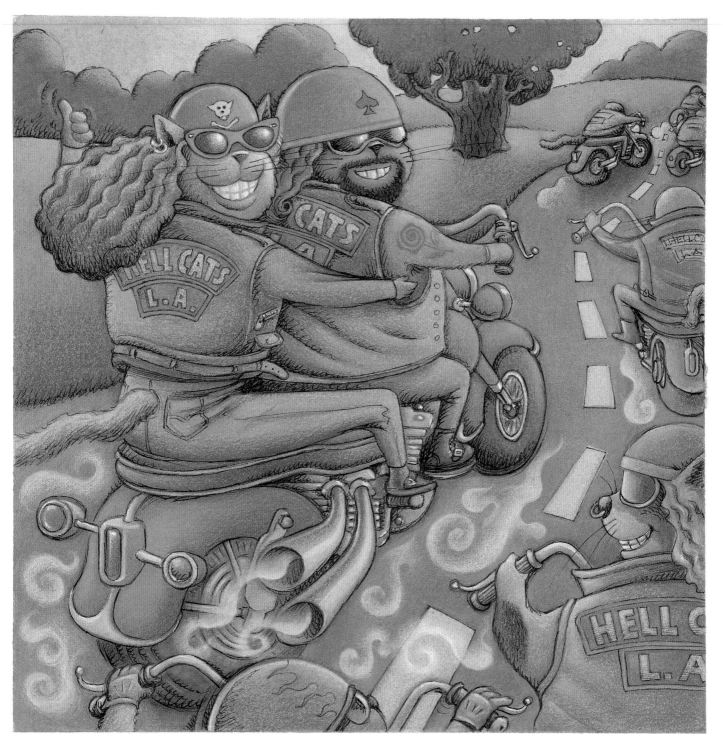

SOLUTION Engage in life affirming experiences

BIBLIOGRAPHY

{BOOKS}

Barbach, L. **The Pause: Positive Approaches To Menopause** New York: Dutton, 1993

Becker, S. **All I Need To Know I Learned From My Cat.** New York: Workman, 1990

Bicks, J.R. **The Revolution In Cat Nutrition.** New York: Rawson Associates, 1986.

Budoff, P.W. **No More Hot Flashes, And Other Good News.** New York: Putnam, 1983.

Diagram Group. **Guide a su Gato.** Barcelona: Juan Granica, 1983.

Camuti, L. **Park Avenue Vet.** New York: Holt, Rinehart and Winston, 1962.

Cole, C. **A Cat's Body.** New York: Morrow, 1982.

Cutler, W. **Menopause, A Guide For Women And The Men Who Love Them.** New York: Norton, 1983.

Guggisberg, C.A.W. **Wild Cats of the World.** New York: Taplinger Publishing Co., 1975

McMorrow, F. **Midolescence: The Dangerous Years.** New York: Quadrangle/
New York Times Book Co., 1974.

Milari, M. **The Body Language and Emotion of Cats.** New York: Norton, 1987.

{BOOKS}

Perry, S. **Natural Menopause: The Complete Guide to a Women's Most Misunderstood Passage.**
Reading, MA: Addison-Wesley Publishing Co., 1992.

Platt, C. **How To Be A Happy Cat.** Pittstown, NJ: Main Street Press, 1987.

Randolph, E. **How To Be Your Cat's Best Friend.** Boston: Little, Brown, 1981.

Ransahoff, R. **Venus After Forty: Sexual Myths, Men's Fantasies, and Truths About Middle-Aged Women.** Far Hills, NJ: New Horizon Press, 1987.

Sand, G. **Is It Hot In Here Or Is it Me?** New York: HarperCollins, 1993

Sumrall, A., and Taylor, D., editors. **Women of the 14th Moon: Writings on Menopause.**
Freedom, CA: Crossing Press, 1991.

Taber, G. **Conversations With Amber.** Philadelphia: Lippincott, 1978.

Van Vechten, C. **The Tiger In The House.** New York: Bonanza Books, 1936.

Walker, W. **A Study of the Cat With Reference To Human Beings.**
Philadelphia: Saunders College Publishing, 1982.

{ARTICLES}

Barlow, D. **"Managing the Menopause: From Pumpkins to HRT."** The Lancet July 10 '93 p66(2)

Braus, P. **"Facing Menopause."** American Demographics March '93 p44(5)

Butcher, L. **"A Cats-Only Clinic? It's About Time, The Patients Purr."**
The Kansas City Business Journal May 29 '92 p1(2)

Caras, R. **"The Hidden Life of Cats."** Washingtonian May '94 p70(5)

Coudert, J. **"What I Learned From My Cats."** Woman's Day Oct 13 '92 p80(3)

Gutfeld, G., Rao, L. and Sangiorgio, M. **"Relax The Flash."** Prevention Mar '93 p18(1)

Lamott, A. **"Who Killed Cock Robin?"** California July '89 p15(2)

Laycock, J. **"Cougars In Conflict."** Audubon March '88 p86(9)

Miller, L. **"Older Pets Need Special Care."** Pet Product News April '93 p50(1)

O'Shea, C. **"The Secrets of Highly Successful Cats."** Good Housekeeping Jan '95 p134(1)

Rosen, F. **"Love Him, Love His Cat."** Cosmopolitan Nov '94 p92(2)

Seligman, J. **"Every Woman for Herself."** Newsweek May 25 '92 p80(2)

Spake, A. **"The Raging Hormone Debate."** Health Jan-Feb '94 p46(10)

Weber, S. **"The Pause That Refreshes."** Vegetarian Times Feb '94 p112(1)

OTHER BOOKS OF INTEREST
FOR WOMEN AND THEIR CATS

The Menopause Self-Help Book by Susan Lark, M.D.

A woman's guide to feeling wonderful for the second half of her life, this book is the first completely practical, all-natural master plan for relieving and preventing every symptom of menopause. *224 pages*

The Women's Health Companion by Susan Lark, M.D.

The first book of its kind to provide information, menus, meal plans and recipes for specific health issues confronting women, while remaining beneficial for the entire family. *350 pages*

Why Cats Paint by Heather Busch and Burton Silver

Should the marks a cat makes be treated as art, or are they simply forms of territorial behavior? This book is an unprecedented photographic record of cat creativity that will intrigue art- and cat-lovers alike. *96 pages*

The Kama Sutra for Cats by Burton Silver and Margaret Woodhouse

Practical but whimsical, this instructive, illustrated gift book explains perplexing phenomena observed regularly by cats, in the form of an ancient text. *72 pages*

The Tao of Meow {Life's Little Instruction Book Fur Cats} by Margaret Gee and John Woodhouse

Cats live by a different code than their human companions, and we rarely have an insight into why they do what they do. This manual of good behavior for cats is charmingly illustrated and intended to inspire good thoughts and kind acts. *64 pages*

Available from your local bookstore, or order direct from the publisher.
Call or write for our catalogs of over 400 books, posters, and tapes.

Ten Speed Press and Celestial Arts
Box 7123, Berkeley, California 94707
Order phone {800} 841-2665; FAX {510} 559-1629